The Hidden Power of Employee Happiness

or

Happiness Achieves Employee Excellence

Authored by

Michael Bridgman

Copyright © 2017 Michael Bridgman

All rights reserved.

ISBN-10:1547055421

ISBN-13:9781547055425

© Michael Bridgman

DEDICATION

This book is dedicated to everyone that has made my life so incredibly fulfilling. I have received extraordinary love and support from my family, friends, employees, and coworkers throughout my life. It has been their love and support along with my spiritual connection to the loving Creator of all life itself that has inspired me and made this book possible.

© Michael Bridgman

This book may not be reproduced in any form, in whole or in part, without written permission from Michael Bridgman. It's easy to get permission. Just email bridgman302@gmail .com and ask.

This publication is designed to provide information on the author's actual experience. It is sold with the understanding that the author is not engaged in rendering legal, accounting, or other professional advice. The author and/or publisher do not guarantee that anyone following these techniques, suggestions, tips, ideas, or strategies will be successful. The author and/or publisher shall have neither liability nor responsibility to anyone with respect to any loss or damage caused, or alleged to be caused, directly or indirectly by the information contained in this book. If legal advice or other expert assistance is required, the services of a competent professional should be sought. The author and publisher shall not be liable for your misuse of this material. This book is strictly for entertainment and informational purposes only.

© 2017 Michael Bridgman All Rights Reserved

© Michael Bridgman

Preface

"I've learned that people will forget what you said, people will forget what you did, but people will never forget how you made them feel."

Maya Angelou

Far too many companies do not get the best performance out of their employees. It seems that there are employees everywhere who are unhappy and simply don't care about the success of their employer. They need a job and an income, so they stick with it.

Working with more than 125 companies as an employee, consultant, and on temporary assignment, it has become obvious to me that the most important factor concerning a company's success is how that company

© Michael Bridgman

values their employees. Companies that value their employees and express their appreciation have a much better opportunity to succeed. Companies that don't value their employees tend to limit their success opportunities. Management with many of today's companies use a "you have to do it because I say so" set of rules. Punishment for rule violations is touted as the best motivator. Management may feel a sense of control, but invariably the results are often high turnover, low productivity, and deficient customer service.

I have learned that as human beings, we are consistently influenced by our emotions. Both happiness and unhappiness are often the result of emotional reactions to circumstances. No one I know likes to be unhappy. Since people prefer to be happy they want to stay

© Michael Bridgman

where they find happiness. When a company creates a happiness culture that results in a happy workplace, the opportunities for company success becomes transformational.

Below are five fundamentals that I have learned that should help provide for happy employees.

1. A sense of accomplishment.

2. Fellowship that results from shared goals.

3. Teamwork where people interact in support of each other.

4. Being respected.

5. Pride in the company and the company's mission.

© Michael Bridgman

Content

Chapters

© Michael Bridgman

© Michael Bridgman

Introduction

"When we share our story, it opens up our hearts for other people to share their stories. And it gives us the sense that we are not alone on this journey." Janie Shepherd

"If a goal is worth pursuing, it's a goal worth telling others about. There's no such thing as a silent dream." John Maxwell

Experience has been my greatest teacher. So, by sharing my personal experiences with you, it is my thought that you may be able to use and apply the knowledge I have attained to your own life and accomplishments. For example, I learned that

© Michael Bridgman

humans will often respond predictably to conditions. The best way to change behavior is to change conditions. When you analyze behavior, you need to examine the situations that are causing both the good and bad behavior. I have also learned that behavior is mostly induced by emotions. Emotions are feelings and it is our feelings that cause us to react to circumstances. However, I must also add that our reactions to circumstances are a choice regardless of how we feel. The Greek philosopher Epictetus asserted, *"it's not what happens to you that matters, but how you react to it that matters."*

When people adapt the right behavior in their lives, they enjoy life more both on and off the job. Believe it or not, I had an employee that told me he enjoyed being on the job with

© Michael Bridgman

his coworkers more than he did being at home. The good feelings that come from accomplishment, fellowship, and teamwork brought about a happiness that my employees did not always find outside of the job.

This book is not intended to be an autobiography but rather a compilation of how I have lived my life and the actions I have taken to make the most of it. My consideration is that when you get to know what I have been through, you will be able to parallel my experiences with your own. We all experience life's ups and downs and you will find that I've certainly had my share. I have been treated unfairly by a few people and I have been treated extremely well by others. With all I have been through both good and bad, I've learned two very important lessons. Lesson

© Michael Bridgman

one, is that what we give to others is what we get back. Our actions come back to us just like a reflection from a mirror. Lesson two, is that life is a result of our choices and the choices we make are what give us the life we live.

Hopefully, my story will give you your own personal perspective on how to apply my experiences to your own circumstances.

This is not a book of instruction with a guaranteed result. I am simply offering ideas and suggestions derived from my own personal experience that when applied have provided the same consistently successful results that I have enjoyed.

On October 17, 1978, I incorporated Brio Industries as a specialty contractor providing above grade high rise sidewall and parking

© Michael Bridgman

deck waterproofing including high rise roofing. This work was performed primarily on five story and above concrete constructed commercial buildings and multi-story parking garages. The work involved caulking, window spline glazing, expansion joint rebuilding, concrete repair, elastomeric coatings and various roofing systems. Everything we did was specific to the job and required a high level of training and strict adherence to the job specifications.

Starting out was difficult, as it is for most new businesses. The two most critical problems were finding responsible workers and the ability to buy the required liability insurance. My employees were awful. I had problems of tardiness, pilferage, and negligent work performance. Counseling didn't help and

13

© Michael Bridgman

their continued bad behavior was going to put me in danger of going out of business. Originally, I felt I had no choice except to terminate the ones causing the problems. Then I realized that just firing people wasn't the answer since I could not hire all perfect employees to replace them. Hiring was a very time consuming and expensive process and I could not spend all my time hiring and training new people. So, I concluded that the only viable solution was to change the bad behavior to good behavior with my existing employees.

While I was trying to overcome employee problems, I also had to deal with the problem of getting required liability insurance. I could not find an insurance company that was willing to provide the required liability insurance. An agent told me that I was rejected

14

© Michael Bridgman

since insurance companies did not know how to rate me because I was performing a specialized type of work that the insurance companies had limited underwriting experience with. Also, they were concerned that I was new in business.   Large jobs required liability insurance and without it I would not be able to get any contracts for the larger jobs. Finally, after a month of seeking out agents and applying to a dozen insurance companies, I finally found an insurance company willing to work with me. They would sell me the needed liability insurance by the job for one month at a time. With the month to month coverage, I had the threat of not being renewed at the end of every month. Plus, not having annual liability insurance meant that I was unable to bid on any long-term jobs.

15

© Michael Bridgman

Unknown risk was the problem with the insurance companies and that meant that safety was paramount. I had to show insurance companies that there really was no risk. Safety was essential for the workers hanging on swing scaffolding on the side of the buildings as well as for the pedestrians walking below. So first and foremost, I had to develop a culture of safety with the employees. But, what was the best way to develop the culture I needed?

I remembered how I had been successful in sales by developing relationships with my customers. So, relationship building with my employees might be the answer.

In the beginning of my sales career, I learned that to make sales you had to develop

© Michael Bridgman

the confidence of the customer. To develop the confidence with the customer you had to cultivate a positive mindset about the product and what the product would do for them. I knew how positive mindsets are fostered through friendly relationships. I also learned that people will buy from people they trust and have confidence in more often than they will buy from a company or a brand.

As my relationship building skills increased my sales increased. As a result of relationship building, I achieved exceptional sales results with three well known international companies. Top company salesperson worldwide at 260% of quota with an international appliance manufacturer. Top salesperson in the Mid-Atlantic Region and after promotion, the top key area manager in

© Michael Bridgman

the eastern division with another international appliance manufacturer. The largest territorial sales increase in the company at 230% with an international rent a car company. There were several factors that go into reaching these sales levels, such as dependability, good communication and excellent customer service, but most importantly for me they were all built around developing friends through shared relationships. Relationship building has been the most important success factor for me in both sales and management throughout my life. Surprisingly, you really do get back from people what you give to them.

So, knowing how the influence of relationships gave me extraordinary sales results, I set out to develop a company culture within my waterproofing company by using

18

© Michael Bridgman

relationships as the foundation for developing a safety and work performance culture. We are all different with different core values and behavior. So, when you have a group of employees and you apply a group centered behavior, the employee mindset becomes focused on the group dynamics and not on the individual self. By making people aware of how their mindset creates their actions, their actions create their results, and how everything they do affects someone else, the workers began to understand the importance of their actions and their relationships with each other.

Once I had all the employees working together with supporting relationships for doing everything the right way, their work performance improved to outstanding levels.

19

© Michael Bridgman

When people are of the same mind, it becomes transformational. Costs went down and productivity went up. Because of our safety and work performance along with four jobsite inspections by the insurance company, I was offered annually renewable general liability insurance after the first six months. Annually renewable liability insurance now allowed me to bid on much larger long-term jobs.

In summary, everything we do not only shapes our own life, but what we do also has a direct effect on the lives of those close to us and shapes their lives as well. My hope is that the book will inspire people to live a better life filled with satisfaction, happiness, and love for themselves, as well as their families and their

© Michael Bridgman

fellow humans. Remember, we are not alone on this planet.

I personally believe that life is a gift from God and how we live that life is our gift back to God. Throughout my life, I have always wanted to make the most of that wonderful gift.

Thank you for your interest and enjoy.

Mike Bridgman,

Email - bridgman302@gmail.com.

© Michael Bridgman

Chapter One

My Early Accomplishments Using the

Power of Relationships

"You can make more friends in two months by becoming interested in other people than you can in two years by trying to get other people interested in you."– Dale Carnegie

"Many relationship problems are rooted in a communication breakdown. These can be as simple as not really hearing what the other person is saying, because we get caught up in our own fixed perspectives."- Sumesh Nair

© Michael Bridgman

I have a characteristically outgoing personality and have always found it easy to develop good relationships with people. That ability helped me early on when I began my business experience in 1965 after serving three years active duty in the US Navy. Washington, DC had been my prior duty station and I knew that the DC area was an excellent place to find a good job. So, I returned to DC and began my first job with a finance company. However, the nineteen sixties were a time when there was a lot of job opportunities in commission sales and I felt I could make more money in sales. So, I moved on to my first commission sales job at a downtown Washington, DC, furniture and appliance retail store. The store management did not allow customers to roam about the store unescorted so customers were

© Michael Bridgman

assigned to a salesperson. Salespeople would wait at the entrance. As the customers came in, they would be assigned by a receptionist to the salesperson at the front of the wait line and the sales person stayed with the customer until the customer left. There were five very large floors of furniture and appliances so most of the customers appreciated having an escort to show them where everything was located.

I thrived right from the start and attribute my success to asking the customer a lot of questions. People like to talk about themselves, so I would ask a few questions about what kind of job they had, where they lived, and where they grew up. (Washington, DC is a transient area and most people are from somewhere else so it is rare to find a local born native). I was also very thorough about asking

© Michael Bridgman

questions about what they wanted, how they wanted to use it, where it was going to fit in their home, and what styles they liked. I was always very professional and would back off without losing my consideration of being helpful if it appeared they did not like too many questions. Since it was always my desire to be helpful, I needed answers to better understand how to help. The way I used the ask questions approach made it easy to develop rapport.

By the second month, I was earning more than twice the money I had been paid at my prior salaried position with the consumer finance company. I was single at the time and the money I was making allowed me to afford the good life which I enjoyed immensely.

© Michael Bridgman

After being on the job for four months, one of my credit denied customers, who were young newlyweds, came in to thank me for selling them their three rooms of furniture and wanted to show me pictures of how nice their apartment looked. It was a nice gesture and I ended up selling them a lamp. But I knew from my commission statement that they had originally been credit denied which meant the sale was canceled and I lost my commissions. I decided to do some checking. After checking, I found out that about a third of my sales that had been credit denied were being rewritten with new credit approval by another salesman. There was an obvious collusion perpetrated against me by the credit manager and the salesman. The credit manager and the salesman were literally taking commissions

26

© Michael Bridgman

that I had previously earned and putting the money in their pockets. I guess because I was the young new kid, I was unable to get any support from the store owners to protect the sales that were being taken away from me. So, I felt that I had no choice except to leave.

I went on to take a salaried sales position with an international rent a car company. This was an excellent job, and after my second year I had the largest territorial sales increase in the company. However, the company had a structured pay schedule for each position or pay grade with no bonus structure and without any pay incentive for results. I had received three small pay raises, but what disappointed me was that I could not receive pay raises proportionate to the increased sales income I brought to the company. The only path to

© Michael Bridgman

higher income was to move up to a higher management position. So, I left the rent a car company to return to a commission job knowing I would be paid in direct proportion to my sales. The good news is because of my proven successful retail furniture and appliance sales experience, I found another commission sales job selling wholesale appliances to retail stores as a manufacturer's representative. I continued to do extremely well with my first manufacturer's rep. job and became top salesman in the Mid-Atlantic region at the end of my first year. My success was a direct result of the relationships I built with my client store managers, buyers, and most importantly the salespeople on the floor. The buyers and store managers would buy the appliances that sold. Of course, the more the

© Michael Bridgman

salespeople sold the more the managers bought. So, most of my time and effort was spent with the store's floor salespeople who did the actual selling. My process was to make sure they had full and complete product knowledge along with sales techniques.

One of the many successful sales techniques I used was to teach the salespeople how to ask questions to find the buyers real reason for making a purchase and then shape the sales pitch into meeting the need that the customer said they wanted. The "ask questions to sell" was developed from my original approach to being helpful that I used with my first commission sales job at the furniture store. When properly used, asking questions is very effective in building rapport and strengthening the relationship with the

© Michael Bridgman

customer. The customer recognizes that you are genuinely interested in making certain that they will be happy with their purchase.

I learned that people do not buy appliances but buy what the appliance will do for them. For example, a customer coming in for a basic toaster could end up buying a toaster/broiler oven when the salesperson asked the right questions. Asking questions is also useful in overcoming the "I am just looking" syndrome. The ask questions technique was very successful and highly valued by the floor salespeople.

I also set weekly goals for the salespeople to win a free steak dinner for two at a well-known DC area restaurant chain. Everyone could win if they met the goals. The steak dinner

© Michael Bridgman

vouchers worked extremely well. I purchased the vouchers from the restaurant chain's promotions department at a discounted price of $5.00 with a value of $15.00. In 1969, $15.00 paid for a premium steak dinner for two, complete with house wine or draft beer and desert. So ultimately, I had many store salespeople increasing sales of my products and eating well with their significant other. If there were several winners in a store, they would sometimes enjoy their steak dinner as a group. As a result, everything I was doing created many friendships and the salespeople sold my products because of that friendship. Since none of my competitor's sales reps were doing what I was doing, my products were outselling all the others by a large margin. By the way, the individual sales goals I set for

© Michael Bridgman

each salesperson to get a steak dinner were worth $50.00 in commissions for me and about $300.00 in commissions for the salesperson. I was only giving up 10% of my commissions or $5.00 for the steak promotion. Keep in mind that $300.00 extra income each month was the equivalent of a well above average weeks' pay in 1969/1970. My steak promotions provided the incentive for the store salespeople to make that extra $300.00, because they made more sales during the promotion than they did without the promotion. Competition for the steak dinners among the sales people turned out to be an excellent motivator. It was a win-win for everyone.

In late December, the buyer for one of my appliance retailers with had a chain of nine

© Michael Bridgman

super stores, knew that I was likely to win the top salesman award. So, as a favor to me he ordered two truckloads of product just to make certain I would go over the top. Those two truckloads turned out to be the largest single order of the year for a territory representative and assured my position as top salesperson in the eastern division.

Promotions with the company were based on sales performance, so as result of my sales success I was promoted to key area manager. As a manager, my commission earnings were based on overrides from the five salespeople that I managed. This meant that I was no longer in direct control of my income. Thinking I could get the same sales results out of my five salespeople that I had been able to achieve for myself, I expected my income to grow even

33

more. However, my expectations were unrealistic for several reasons but mostly because of my inexperience with managing people. My biggest problem was that I was ineffective in getting my salespeople to use the same sales techniques that I had used, even though they were proven successful. It is interesting that I could achieve better results and more cooperation with my customer's retail floor salespeople than I could obtain from the people that worked for me. After all, I was their boss. I learned the hard way that people will do what they want, not necessarily what they are told to do especially independent thinking commission salespeople.

So, my income as a manager turned out to be less than I had earned as a salesperson which was very disappointing. It was after this

© Michael Bridgman

failed management experience that I began my quest to study how to manage employees. I knew the importance of building relationships but I did not know how to inspire the people that worked for me. I found that people need an incentive to achieve anything and money is not a sufficient motivator like it was with me.

In the meantime, along came a rival appliance manufacturer that was not established with the major dealers that were my customers. I was ready made for this rival company to help bring their products into the major department, chain, and catalogue stores that were my current customers. So, this company made me an offer I could not refuse. The commission percentage was double what I had been paid as a salesperson with my current employer. Since I already had devoted

35

© Michael Bridgman

relationships with my customers their offer was simply too good to turn down. I called on all the same buyers, store managers, and store salespeople with a matching product line while offering better profit margins along with the same marketing, training, and advertising support. I also convinced some of the store management to provide a small bonus commission for their store salespeople known as a spiff. The spiff replaced my steak dinners since the restaurant chain no longer offered the discounted vouchers and I was unable to find a restaurant chain that had a similar type of promotion. The spiff was helpful, but I can tell you first hand that money by itself is not nearly as good of an incentive as a gift of something tangible, especially a gift that has good memories attached to it like the steak

© Michael Bridgman

dinners offered. However, the steak dinners had been so well appreciated that they had a lingering effect helping to maintain the loyalty from the store salespeople. This lingering effect recalls the quote from Maya Angelou on the back cover. It seems that people really don't forget how you made them feel, especially when it is a good feeling.

I succeeded in making the switch work mostly due to the loyalty of my customers and quickly became the top salesman in the company worldwide. I was making more money than my neighbor who was a vice president at a bank. I was also making more money than the company's two layers of management above me. However, it seems greed took a front seat because of my success. My two managers cut my commission from 6% to 3%. The

© Michael Bridgman

justification my managers used for the commission cut was that I should still be happy, since that even with the cut I was still making more money than any other sales representative in the company and the 3% commission was an industry standard. By the way, the 3% my managers took from me went right into their pockets.

I was a contract sales representative and not an employee of the company, so I took my contract to a lawyer. The lawyer agreed that they clearly violated the contract and legally my commission could not be cut without prior written approval of both parties. My lawyer sent a letter to the company president since he was the signatory on the contract. When my two managers found out about the letter to the president, they promptly fired me. The contract

38

© Michael Bridgman

did have a cancelation clause that could be exercised by either party at any time with written notice.

Fortunately, I did get all my back commissions due from the time of the cut to the time of discharge. Then the company and my two managers found out what I already knew. My success was a result of loyal customers which were buying from me and not from the company. In other words, the products did not sell on their own. My previous managers had replaced me with a salaried sales representative who was given instructions to do everything the same way I had been doing it. However, the salaried rep did not do everything I had been doing. As an example, my replacement did not spend any time with the store salespeople during high

© Michael Bridgman

store traffic times on nights and weekends. Because of the absence of support and continued relationships, sales dropped off substantially. Within six months, the salaried rep and both of my prior managers were fired as a consequence of the decline in sales. Their greed came back to bite them and it cost everyone involved. Unfortunately, my managers failed to see that my success was their success and by sabotaging me they sabotaged their selves.

The same day I was fired, I was offered a sales representative's job with the trucking company that was providing the distribution services for the appliance manufacturer where I had just been fired from. This job provided a company car and expenses with a good salary. It did not give me the opportunity of an

40

© Michael Bridgman

unlimited income as I had in my previous commission jobs. Also, the salary was substantially less than I had been making, but it was a job that I could start immediately. So, I took it. I also have had a fascination with the trucking industry since I was a little kid.

I have always been dedicated to my jobs and take my responsibilities very seriously. So, I was fully committed to selling trucking and distribution services. I learned as much as I could about the trucking industry. I attended community college taking a transportation curriculum and joined the Sales and Marketing Council of the American Trucking Associations, the Maryland Motor Truck Association, and the Delta nu Alpha transportation fraternity. After four months of learning, growing, and making sales, I was

© Michael Bridgman

promoted to sales manager. As manager in addition to sales, I oversaw customer service with the terminal managers and I represented the company in teamster negotiations.

However, I had a problem because I had to answer to a vice president who I felt restricted my ability to develop new business. He did not want me to spend money on lunches or take time to just stop by and talk with potential customers. He expected me to meet with current customers when there was a problem and did not want me wasting time with potential customers unless they were seeking an active bid. But of course, without building the relationships with the potential customers, I never got the invitations to bid. I have always been results oriented. Since I felt that my vice president prevented me from getting the

© Michael Bridgman

results I knew I could get without his restrictions, I decided to leave the trucking company.

I went back to a commission job selling for a company that manufactured vehicle activity recording instruments for the transportation industry called a tachograph. A tachograph was a mechanical forerunner to the electronic computers that are used today. The mechanical tachograph records vehicle motion activity with event actuated marking needles on a clock driven paper disk.

This job kept me in the trucking industry, which for some unknown reason I have always loved. I was also able to stay in touch with many of the industry contacts I had developed from my past job with the trucking company.

© Michael Bridgman

Sadly, I should have expected what was going to happen next based on my experience with the appliance company. For two years, I was doing well opening new accounts, and selling products to trucking companies, bus companies, and police departments while making good money. Once again, I unexpectedly experienced the same assault on my success as before.

The last straw was having two major federal government accounts taken away from me just prior to when these two accounts were ready to close on very large sales. I was called into the instrument company president's office and told that these two accounts were too large for a single sales rep to manage and the accounts needed to become company accounts so better service could be provided. As a token for losing

44

© Michael Bridgman

the accounts, the company offered me a salary of $20,000 plus bonus with company car and expenses. A potential income of $35,000 per year was possible which was about the same that I was making in commissions. The real kicker was that I would have to give up over $60,000.00 in first year commissions. The $18,000 commission with one of the government accounts was from an initial order of $225,000 that was budgeted to become over $2,000,000 over the next year. This account alone would have paid me an additional $160,000 in commissions the next year after the initial sale. The order for the other government account was about $525,000. With my help this sale was fully funded from a supporting federal agency and was worth $42,000 in commissions. Bottom line is that

© Michael Bridgman

combined I was told I would have to give up $220,000 in commissions over the next two years in exchange for an annual salary of $20,000 with a potential $15,000 annual bonus with a company car and expenses. There was no negotiation for these commissions and their offer of a company car and salary plus bonus was a take it or leave it offer. So, I felt I had no choice but to quit.

Regrettably for the company they had no idea of the relationships I had to build with many people over a year and a half to put these two sales together. To develop these two large sales, I had filled out substantial paperwork for federal sole source funding and put together a complete program of installation and training which included instructional support for ongoing information processing

© Michael Bridgman

derived from the recordings. The instructional support was an important essential to the sales.

After I quit, guess what? Apparently, the company felt the sales were in the bag and failed to follow up properly with the supervising chiefs that oversaw the programs. Consequently, these two federal government agencies lost confidence in the company. Each of the program chiefs called me to verify that I would no longer be their sales representative. Now that I was out of the picture the confidence they had in the company and the programs was lost. They were both concerned about the technical aspects of utilizing the recorded data and not having my after-sale support. They both told me that these projects were too big to take chances with. Because of

© Michael Bridgman

their concerns over the after sale support they both decided to cancel their purchases. Once again, greed cost everyone.

To this day, I am truly amazed at the ignorance of a large international instrument company and how they underestimated the complexities involved in the sale. For me, it was largely about relationship building and somehow relationship building was completely missing in their thought process. Apparently, they thought that because they were the sole provider and the sales were fully funded that the sales were "in the bag." They lost sight of the fact that people buy from people more often than they buy from companies, especially in complex sales where critical service is important.

© Michael Bridgman

© Michael Bridgman

Chapter Two

My Own Business

Brio Industries Incorporated

"Dictionary is the only place that success comes before work. Hard work is the price we must pay for success. I think you can accomplish anything if you're willing to pay the price"

Vince Lombardi

"The people who get on in this world are the people who get up and look for the circumstances they want, and, if they can't find them, make them."

George Bernard Shaw

© Michael Bridgman

At this point I have had it! I decided that the only way I could keep from being the victim of other people's greed was to be my own boss in my own business. So, I started Brio Industries as a contractor in the business of high rise (five stories and above) waterproofing along with parking deck waterproofing. Later, we expanded to provide high-rise roofing. Many established roofing companies cannot find employees that are willing to work on the roof of a twenty-story building with no parapet wall. Apparently, there must be roofers that are afraid of heights?

I chose this field because at the time waterproofing was a needed service with recently built buildings and there were not many companies providing this type of highly specialized work. This was during a period of

51

© Michael Bridgman

active commercial development. Because of new architectural designs and construction methods, there were numerous waterproofing related deficiencies, especially with concrete constructed high rise buildings. It is interesting to note that the average age of the buildings I worked on was about five years old. The five years seemed to be the amount of time that it took for litigation between the building owners, the architects, engineers, and construction companies to reach a settlement on the amount of money needed to rectify the deficiencies. I was often paid from these settlements. Once all the settlements were resolved, I could start work. So, I learned everything I could about concrete repair, caulking, sealing, window and panel systems, expansion joint rebuilding, spline glazing, and

© Michael Bridgman

high-rise roofing. I had a saying back then "if they built buildings the way they should have, I would not have a business."

Right from the start the employees were very difficult to control. I wanted a successful business and knew it was impossible to hire all perfect people. So, I felt that the only choice I had was to change the conduct of my existing employees into the responsible dedicated workers that I needed to be successful. I started my quest to develop my employees by using what I had learned from reading books on management by such authors as Peter Drucker, Zig Zigler, John C. Maxwell, Tom Peters, Dale Carnegie, and so on.

The information from the books I had read was a good base to get me started. But I

© Michael Bridgman

quickly learned that establishing employee cooperation is not a simple follow the book type of task. For more than two years I tried many different types of rationales to discover what worked and what did not work. Once I found what worked, I stayed with the proven methods while continuing to build on the new methods that were providing the desired results. Ultimately, I fostered loyal, dedicated and responsible employees. The end results were exceptional. As my employee performance plan continued to mature, improvements were made in responsible employee behavior, quality of work, taking care of equipment, tools, maintenance, and on the job personal appearance. Behavior and appearance were very important because we were working on high rise office buildings using swing

© Michael Bridgman

scaffolding hanging outside the windows of mostly expensive office space. People were constantly watching us work from inside. As I used to tell my workers, that is why our work platforms are called swing staging. "We are on stage."

As an example of the importance of appearance, I was asked to take over and rebid on a contract where a company had been called off the job. The reason this company's contract was terminated was because of one employee. Evidently, there was one employee that refused to pull his pants up. Because he wore his pants too low, he would expose half of his derriere to the people watching from inside when he bent over to pick up items off the floor of the scaffold. The building manager told me that the company's president had been told

© Michael Bridgman

five different times to have his employee wear his pants properly. The complaints from the tenants caused the building owners to hire a lawyer and charge the contractor with "breach of contract" so the contract could be canceled. It seems that people don't want to see a fat man's half exposed rear end when looking out of the window.

It has often been said, "it all starts with attitude." One of my approaches to improve attitude was using a method of give and take. I bought them the best equipment and tools available to make their job easier and safer and they in turn gave me their best effort to use the equipment and tools properly. I bought sectional scaffolding with built-in adjustable railings and nonskid floors with kick plates. This scaffolding was three times the cost of the

© Michael Bridgman

cheaper ladder boards with long pipe-tubes for railings. I bought instant locking safety rope grabs instead of the cheaper friction type of rope grab that allowed the person to fall up to fifteen feet before the grab would stop a fall. I also provided everyone with a full body harness, identical to a parachute harness, instead of a simple safety belt that could break a back or allow a person to slide through during a fall.   Without saying anything to my workers, they responded to my effort in providing the best for them with a sense of obligation to give me their best. As an example, we often had to remove old caulk and replace it with new caulk on many of our jobs. Removing old caulk can be very difficult because it is often hard and brittle and sticks to the

© Michael Bridgman

substrate so it must be scraped off after it has been cut out.

The common tools for doing this work are a hooked carpet cutting knife, a putty knife, and paint scraper. Using these three tools made caulk removal very labor intensive. I always wanted to provide the best tools available for my employees. So, when I was at the "World of Concrete" industry trade show in Las Vegas, I was looking over the displays and saw an electric caulk cutting knife. The electric caulk cutting knife was marketed as the only one made and sold for $350.00. It came with eight different blades to be used for different types of caulk and substrates and was packaged in a durable storage case. It was obvious to me that this electric caulk cutting

© Michael Bridgman

knife was a very well designed high-quality specialty tool that could save my workers a lot of time and trouble. So, I bought one on the spot.

Later, while walking through the display aisles I met up with my carpet knives supplier. I proudly told him that I purchased an electric caulk cutting knife. The supplier said that he had seen it and was not interested because it was too expensive for his customers. He also said that I was nuts to pay that kind of price when I could get a whole case of 144 carpet cutters for $85.00, which was a quarter of the cost of the electric knife. He also felt that my workers would not take care of the electric knife and it would not last a month. Guess what! He was wrong on all counts. The workers

© Michael Bridgman

loved the electric knife and the labor savings paid for it in just the first two weeks of use. I was also able to buy replacement blades from the manufacturer. The electric knife I originally bought lasted for ten years of regular use and was still working at the time I sold the assets of the company. This electric knife is a great example of a win for the workers and a win for the company.

Two thirds of our contracts were out of town which required my employees to be away from home. So, in this respect, I had limited control because they usually worked and played as a group. In many ways, this made managing more difficult since I had to watch over their off-duty behavior in addition to supervising their work. I did not want anyone

© Michael Bridgman

coming to work the next day hungover and without sufficient sleep, which was common place before I succeeded with the group centered sense of responsibility. Once the group centered sense of responsibility was accepted by everyone, the employees self-enforced their own behavior on and off the job. Responsibility became an attitude because an attitude becomes a way of life.

No two jobs were the same. Every building is different in construction and design and required different repair materials and methods of application. High rise sidewall waterproofing is complex from an engineering point of view and can involve various combinations of caulking, concrete coating, concrete repair, spline glazing, installation of

© Michael Bridgman

expansion joints, and roofing. Buildings had to be rigged with swing scaffold using setup procedures that were unique to each building.

Because of all the complexities involved, I started all jobs with an onsite work assessment meeting with my supervisors to establish the how and why everything had to be done a certain way. This was followed up with a launch dinner with the startup team, usually at a family pizza restaurant. By the way, I would have taken them to any restaurant they wanted but they preferred the casual family atmosphere of a good Italian pizza type restaurant. It seems that pizza and beer were there favorite foods.

Having the whole team of workers involved in the planning process gave them a sense of

© Michael Bridgman

ownership in the job. This enhanced cooperation and eliminated the resistance inherent in some people to be disagreeable about how the work should be performed. After all the details of the action plan were agreed upon by everyone, I would spend two or three days working side by side doing the job with them. This was done to determine the actual methods required for performing how the work needed to be done and to get their approval for work performance and production standards involving all aspects of the job. I called this the commitment phase. After the start up, everyone knew what was expected and the daily production goals were set. Full understanding by everyone involving all aspects of the job was the key. These expectations then became personal goals for

63

© Michael Bridgman

each worker. Daily goals were important even on large jobs that took twelve to eighteen months to complete. Meeting goals day to day gave everyone a feeling of accomplishment and contributed toward a superior work ethic attitude. Everyone focused their effort to stay on the daily goal. If by the end of the week they were sufficiently ahead of the goal, I would let them off early and still pay them for the full day. They really appreciated getting off early on Fridays and the off time I paid them did not cost me extra since the work was progressing within the labor budget including the time off. When everyone knows what to do and focuses on a common group goal with individual performance standards, constant supervision is not needed.

© Michael Bridgman

Most of my contracts were with prestige building owners such as banks, insurance companies, and prominent developers, and included many landmark buildings. So, everyone felt a sense of pride in what they were doing and the importance of doing it right. The pride my workers had because of the importance of our customers added an even higher level of pride and performance. It was like no one wanted to let anyone down either with the company or the clients.

For example, we would notify tenants when we would be working outside their offices a day ahead of time to avoid upsetting anyone seeing us suddenly standing outside their window on the eighteenth floor of an office building. This was especially important when we were working outside the windows of doctors' offices

65

© Michael Bridgman

where patients were being examined and there were no drapes or blinds to block the window because the offices were several stories above ground. The tenant notifications were appreciated by the building management which would from time to time would personally thank my workers for their good work and cooperation with the tenants.

As a method of having my workers and the building management working together, I always introduced my workers to the building manager and his staff to develop a friendly relationship. The result was that building management got to know the workers and in turn we received everyone's cooperation and the opportunity to use the building facilities for material and tool storage, as well as access to the roof.

© Michael Bridgman

The result of the continuous application of the collaborative mindset encouraged higher quality workmanship, increased efficiency, and accountability for profits. Pride in accomplishment brought about job satisfaction which in turn lowered rates of tardiness and turnover. In other words, I succeeded in developing a group of happy, loyal, and dedicated employees striving to do everything the right way.

Along with all the other benefits, we had only one worker's compensation claim and one liability claim both costing less than $15,000 combined during the fourteen-year history of my ownership in the company. These two insurance claims took place early on before I had succeeded in establishing the group centered sense of responsibility that made

© Michael Bridgman

everyone accountable to each other for their actions.

A competitor that tried to build his business by following in my footsteps once asked me, how could I buy the best equipment, hire and keep the best employees, make substantial profits, and stay price competitive? Up until now, I never gave away my secret.

In 1992, I sold the assets of Brio Industries to a large national roofing contractor that wanted to be in the sidewall waterproofing business. I stayed with the purchasing company for nine months as part of the sale to help consolidate Brio's operations into the new company's operations. After the nine months, I reached the point where I had to figure out what I wanted to do with the rest of my life.

© Michael Bridgman

I did not like retirement which I tried for a couple of months, so I went on to work as a business consultant and contract consultant which over time also involved ADA (American's with Disabilities Act) accessibility compliance. This work involved frequent Sunday through Friday travel almost exclusively by air. I enjoyed the travel but never had enough time to sightsee.

© Michael Bridgman

Chapter Three

Living My Childhood Dream to Be a Truck Driver

"A man is not old until regrets take the place of dreams." – John Barrymore

"It is only when we truly know and understand that we have a limited time on earth – and that we have no way of knowing when our time is up – that we will begin to live each day to the fullest, as if it was the only one we had." – Elizabeth Kubler-Ross

After two and a half years, I decided to leave the consulting work and follow a childhood dream. Since I was at a point in life where I

© Michael Bridgman

could do anything I wanted and I had a good understanding of the trucking industry from my time as a trucking company sales manager, I decided to follow my childhood dream and become a professional truck driver. I started as an admissions representative with an accredited truck driving school where I received all my licensing qualifications and went on to become an instructor and director of contract training. The school valued my previous experience as a sales manager with the trucking company along with my transportation studies at a community college, and my prior memberships with national and state trucking associations. The executive director of the school also enjoyed my instruction on transportation history. From a historical point of view the trucking company

© Michael Bridgman

where I had been employed, was founded in 1845. I studied the history of the company and learned a lot about the history of land transportation in the process. I was fascinated with the history of the company from horses and wagons to the evolution of the trucks. Because of its early start, this transportation company was a backdrop for the history of the American trucking industry. This historical knowledge gave me a much broader understanding of the industry than the other instructors since they had been primarily drivers exclusively, so I was chosen to be the instructor for the history lessons.

After six months on the job the owner of the school decided to close the Baltimore, Maryland campus where I worked. So, I looked for a driving job which is what I wanted to do

© Michael Bridgman

from the beginning anyway. But due to my lack of driving experience, I could not find a decent job driving. I already knew the abuse my students received from the companies that hired inexperienced drivers and I did not want to go through what I knew my students had gone through. For the good jobs I needed experience, but how do you get experience if no one will hire you?

My solution was to take a job as a driver for a temporary help agency. I was sent to companies as a temporary driver and my lack of experience never came up as a disadvantage. As it turned out there was one company that requested me every time they needed an outside driver.

© Michael Bridgman

Then eventually that company made me a really great job offer. It was a full-time job as an account support driver going to dedicated contract customers where various supply chain services were provided. These supply chain services could be any combination of trucks and drivers, warehousing, receiving, shipping and order processing. My job was to provide support any way that was needed. My support activities included substitute driving, dispatch, routing, recruiting, training, managing, and anything else that was needed. This was a neat job doing a lot of different things, but the best part for me is that it still involved 40% to 60% driving. Remember I took this job because I wanted to be a truck driver. The driving part is what I have really enjoyed and I must say, driving a big truck all over the

© Michael Bridgman

United States and Canada was a perfect fit for me. The view out of a truck window is a lot more interesting than the view out of the airplane window I had during my consulting assignments.

As a go anywhere, do anything, support team truck driver I was sent on assignments to 87 different dedicated contract companies with a combined 128 locations all throughout the United States and Canada. Many assignments were to first-rate well-run operations with happy employees. To me it was always obvious that when you have happy employees you have excellent operations. However, most often I was sent to companies with operational problems. The most common problem was a shortage of driver's due to high turnover. A lack of qualified drivers often results in delivery

© Michael Bridgman

failures. Just in time delivery requirements for manufacturing operations exacerbates the failed deliveries. I have seen firsthand what can cause excessive turnover, customer service failures, higher equipment maintenance, and accident costs. I found that poor job performance from the employees was mostly the result of employee unhappiness.

On occasion, driver retention difficulties afforded me the opportunity to introduce variations of the employee happiness concepts derived from Brio. In each instance, when the concepts were implemented they were successful in improving working conditions, which in turn lowered operating costs and reduced turnover.

© Michael Bridgman

In June of 2001, I was selected to serve as a Captain on the America's Road Team from June 2001 until June 2003. This is a public outreach program of the American Trucking Association (ATA) and is a high honor bestowed every two years on twelve exceptionally accomplished truck drivers through a competitive selection process. America's Road Team Captains are involved in all sorts of public outreach programs as keynote speakers for public events, local, state and federal level legislative testimony, transportation and supply chain industry conferences and exhibitions, television and radio interviews, and hiring fairs. Because of the public exposure, the America's Road Team is a highly sought after public relations opportunity for the company that has a Road Team Captain.

© Michael Bridgman

However, a certain mid-level manager in my company did not appreciate the public relations opportunity and tried to restrict my participation. Then a management change took place and suddenly I was working for a manager that decided I should have my legs cut out from me completely. He took my salary away from me and put me on hourly pay costing me about a third of my income. Not only that, he also called the America's Road Team Manager and cut me off from any further Road Team involvement. I felt this was a serious mistake for the company from a public relations point of view, but no one was willing to stick their neck out to stop what he was doing. I have a wife and two adult children so for me it was time for a family chat on what to do next. We all agreed that the environment

© Michael Bridgman

was such that I could not stay. So, I put the word out with the Road Team that I was possibly looking for a new position. Fortunately, the vice president of a truckload carrier who served on the ATA executive committee found out that I was looking. He said that he had always wanted an America's Road Team Captain and he would be honored if I would come to work for his company. He made me an offer and I accepted. I would also be fully activated back into Road Team responsibilities.

I was initially hired to be a driver, over the road trainer, and to provide occasional recruiting talks at truck driving schools. I also attended some Road Team events. Well after eight months, the vice president that hired me left the company. Right after he left, my driver

79

© Michael Bridgman

manager stopped paying me for extras such as driver unloads, detention, and extra stops. These payments were clearly spelled out in the driver operations manual and prior to the vice president leaving were never a problem. But my driver manager told me he could not pay me because they were not included in the load preplan. Of course, this excuse is total nonsense. After four weeks of not being paid for the extras, I totaled everything that was due ($600.00+) and filed a request for review with my driver manager's team leader. This caused an immediate repercussion of cuts in miles and delays in reloads plus there was still no meeting scheduled to reach a resolution on my unpaid claims.

While I was having these problems with my driver manager I was also training a student

80

© Michael Bridgman

that was acting in strange ways. He was constantly on his cell phone talking in his native language with what appeared to be a contact of some kind. He would report all activities of the truck such as pickups, load type, delivery schedules, routing, and locations. He would read over in detail all the paperwork and watched in cab communications like a hawk. He was also not at all interested in driving or learning anything about driving. So, I tried to turn him back to the company. Since I was already in hot water they kept telling me to keep working with him. After three weeks, he had lost and repurchased three prepaid cell phones. So, with all this going on, I decided to report him to Highway Watch, which is a Homeland Security program for the trucking industry. I had previously

© Michael Bridgman

received Highway Watch training as part of the America's Road Team commitment. Highway Watch turned me over to the Transportation Security Administration (TSA) where I was assigned an agent. I provided the agent information about my student. My student had damaged my tractor fairings (fairings are air baffle panels on the rear outside corners of the cab) by making turns too tight against the side of the trailer, so I did not allow him to drive any more to avoid further damage.

On the occasion where he crushed the left fairing I had told him to stop three times, stop, stop, stop! Finally, after the damage was done the tractor bound up against the trailer and forced him to stop. I asked him why he didn't stop when I told him? Unbelievably his answer was, *"because I didn't want to."* I had tried all

© Michael Bridgman

my employee management skills on him but could not get any cooperation. Apparently, he was more focused on providing information to the contact on his cell phone instead of becoming a truck driver. Then two days after I had sent my student's information into the TSA agent, I received a call at 1:30 am while waiting at a red-light. I had just picked up a preloaded trailer in Muscatine, IA with office furniture going into Chicago. My student was sitting in the passenger seat. My cell phone *rang* and I answered it with *"hello."* The voice on the other end said, *"your life may be in danger, is he with you?"* I said, *"yes he is sitting in the passenger seat now."* I recognized his voice as the TSA agent. He then said, *"you must get him to a place where the FBI can pick him up as soon as possible."* I had to think

© Michael Bridgman

quickly, so knowing we had a terminal about fifty miles away, I said *"Oh! I don't have enough hours to go into Chicago? I'll go to our terminal in North Liberty, IA, and drop my trailer for relay so I can take time off to recover my hours."* The TSA agent indicated he understood what I met and found the correct address for the terminal.

The agent then said the FBI would meet me there in about two hours. My student was not able to hear the TSA agent over the phone because of the truck noise, so he was not alarmed.

Now, if you are a truck driver reading this you know that trucks are tracked with GPS and as soon as you go off route people back in dispatch panic and want to know what is going

© Michael Bridgman

on. So, I typed a message on the in-cab communications computer that said *"not enough hours to go into Chicago taking load to North Liberty terminal for relay."* I get a message [1]back stating, *"you have enough hours* to go to Chicago, you must deliver load or you will be fired."* I sent a reply that said, *"will not drive illegally taking load to terminal for relay."* I get a message back *"YOU ARE FIRED IF YOU GO TO TERMINAL!!!!."*

My student watched the communication messages very closely and was now concerned that I was going to be fired. But, I told him that a senior safety manager called me about my

---

[1] * The Federal Motor Carrier Safety Administration limits commercial drivers to driving 11 hours per every 24 hours and being on duty no more than 70 hours in an 8-day period. Hours are recovered and become available at midnight every 8 days.

© Michael Bridgman

hours and not to worry about the messages because the person sending them does not know what he is talking about. My student accepted this and went to sleep in the bunk. I arrived at the terminal, parked the trailer in the trailer relay section and then parked the tractor in the bobtail (unhooked tractor) section. My student stayed sleeping in the bunk, so I went inside to meet with the FBI.

After entering the terminal, I looked around for the FBI but they were not there. The only person on duty was the fuel island attendant. I told the attendant what was going on and why I was there. She gave me a quizzical look like I was full of it. It turns out that she had been told to hold me there until the terminal manager arrived so the manager could officially fire me. Apparently, everyone thought I had

© Michael Bridgman

The Hidden Power of Employee Happiness

perpetrated an extraordinary lie to get out of driving in Chicago since no one likes to drive a big truck in all that congestion.

Now keep in mind, I had been with the company for nine months and had a perfect no accident, no complaints, and always on time performance record. But, I guess my story about the FBI etc. was too far over the top for people to believe. I decided to go upstairs to a "quiet room" with comfortable couches and catch a little shut eye. Before I went upstairs, I asked the fuel island attendant to call me when the FBI arrived. Once again, she had a "I don't believe this" look on her face.

Around 7:00 am, I came back down to the driver's lounge at the same time the terminal manager was walking in the door. The FBI was still not there. I told the terminal manager that I needed to talk with him and he told me that it would have to wait until after he finishes an important phone call. He said that people are waiting for his call. The manager then went into his office to make the call. The call lasted about ten minutes and when he finished he called me into his office. It turns out that the important call was all about me. He said to me *"I do not know what is going on. Everyone has always had the highest regard for what you have accomplished but despite your exceptional performance, I have been told that I have to fire you for refusing to drive into Chicago."* I then told him the whole story of what had been going on with the TSA and that I was told the FBI would be coming in to pick up my student (still sleeping in the truck). At this point, I am

© Michael Bridgman

not sure he knew what to believe since he did have a doubtful look on his face.

Later that morning, my student came into the driver's lounge thinking I was recovering my hours so I could drive again. Well about 10:30am, the FBI did show up. They took my student upstairs to interview him and then after two hours took him with them. He was not in hand cuffs and did not appear to be in any distress when they took him. After the FBI left with my student, the terminal manager called me back into the office to tell me I was still fired. Also, he had worked out a deal with my home terminal manager in Pennsylvania to let me take the truck back to where I had my car. This would allow me to remove my personal items (refrigerator, TV, CB radio, clothes, etc.). Otherwise, I would have to

© Michael Bridgman

arrange to have my stuff shipped back to my home. These two managers had to follow their directions in firing me, but at the same time readily went out of their way to make it easier for me to get out of the truck.

My student returned later that evening with the FBI and the company put him with another driver so he could be returned to the company headquarters. I found out the next day from the TSA agent that my student could not be arrested since he had not committed any crimes, but he had given them a lot of information and would be under surveillance.

The next day I picked up a load headed east that would take me to my home terminal in Pennsylvania. I was still fired, but at least I

© Michael Bridgman

had the convenience of removing my belongings directly into my car.

I also had the comfort of knowing that several coworkers with my old employer had been in contact with me, both by email and phone, to convey that they wanted me to come back. The boss that had caused me to leave had been fired and now that he was gone I was welcome to return. Being aware that I could go back to my old job provided the confidence of knowing I had an immediate job waiting. So, I felt that being fired may have been a blessing.

While heading east on the Indiana Toll Road my cell phone rings. Guess who it was? It was the chairman, president, and CEO of the company that was firing me. The first thing he said was, *"I wanted to call you personally and*

© Michael Bridgman

tell you that you are not fired. I would like you to return to headquarters and take you out to lunch if you still want to stay with the company." The president went on to say that he had hired an outside consulting firm to put policies in place to make sure no one else would have to go through what I went through. In closing, he said he would get me back to headquarters next week for the lunch. The president then asked if there was anything else he could do for me. My answer was yes. I told him that I was not getting paid for the extras and that I was owed more than $600.00. I went on to tell him that I could not get a meeting with my driver manager's team leader to resolve the issue. I also mentioned that I am not the only driver with issues about pay and these issues are creating a lot of frustrated

© Michael Bridgman

drivers. This may be one of the reasons he is having 150%+ annual turnover. He said he would personally make sure I was paid, and wanted to discuss any ideas I had at lunch to reduce turnover. I went on to deliver the load I had and went on to pick up and deliver two more loads that routed me to headquarters.

A week later I was sitting in the president's office along with the vice president of operations. We talked about how the drivers were being treated and the three of us agreed that something had to be done to improve driver turnover. The president said that it was costing around $3,400 for every new inexperienced driver they hired. That is a lot of expense when you are hiring sixty drivers per month on average. So, I went over how I created a group of happy dedicated employees

93

© Michael Bridgman

with Brio. I said the first place you must start is to find out from the drivers where the problems are. After the problems are identified, you create the solutions. Then you apply the solutions using a continuous improvement strategy. Once the employees have confidence that their concerns are being addressed you will see their performance improve.

The vice president was very much against having the drivers involved and wanted no more discussion about it. He said "if *you do this you will have the drivers running the company and we will be out of business in no time.*" He went on to say, *"all the drivers need to do is follow orders and make deliveries."* Fortunately, the president did not agree with him and the discussion went on without the participation of the operations vice president.

94

© Michael Bridgman

The president and I continued the discussion. The result was that we would create a new position in the company called a resolution manager. The resolution manager's extension would be the first option on the drivers call in line. Drivers would be assured of confidentiality and be guaranteed that their concern would be addressed personally by the president.

As a side note, the president also made sure that my meeting with my driver manager and team leader was scheduled. Later that afternoon, I had that meeting and received all my back pay with the promise that I would receive all future pay according to the operations manual.

© Michael Bridgman

The next day a senior safety manager was selected to become the resolution manager. He had worked at headquarters for several years and knew the department managers well. He also had the respect of everyone. However, the new resolution manager had no idea of what to do or how to execute the program. So, I talked with him on how to set up the procedures as well as how to handle the calls and ask questions to get the full picture from the driver. I explained how to phrase the questions in such a way that the driver would have confidence that something was really going to be done. I also showed him how to set up a spread sheet for categorizing the different kinds of issues and how to create a trend analysis.

© Michael Bridgman

Each day the resolution manager would report to the president all calls that needed the president's attention so the president could decide what to do. The president then directed the appropriate department manager to fix the problem. After three months, turnover was cut by more than two thirds and accidents were also reduced substantially. I attribute the reduction in accidents to attitude improvement. The program resulted in the drivers being treated with more respect and they no longer had to live with the stress of not knowing what they were getting paid, when they could get home, or how long they would have to wait between loads. Ultimately, the drivers really felt appreciated.

Unfortunately, during the process there was some of the support staff that did not like the

© Michael Bridgman

new empowerment given to the drivers. Some refused to go along and were told to quit or be fired. Several people did leave including my driver manager with almost twenty years of service. Remember? He is the one that had been unwilling to pay me the extras. The success of the resolution manager's program went well beyond anyone's expectation (except mine) and the policy changes made through the program became permanent and, as far as I know, are still in effect today.

Back at my old job it turns out that the boss that took everything away from me was fired seven months after I left. There were several people that wanted me back, so after my old boss had been fired I was getting calls to convince me to return. Finally, after several prior calls, one of my old bosses asked me

© Michael Bridgman

what it would take to get me back. I told him that I wanted to be assigned to the boat account and stay there as long the boat account wanted me. He agreed to it. I stayed on with my current company for another six weeks which was just long enough to be certain that the resolution manager program was well established and providing consistent results. After I left, I continued to stay in touch and made myself available for any questions that might come up.

Upon my return to my old employer and assignment to the boat account, I almost doubled the pay I was getting when I left. All promises were kept and I did get everything I asked for. I also continued to offer suggestions for improvements to operations including conducting driver and management seminars.

© Michael Bridgman

© Michael Bridgman

Chapter Four

What It Takes for Happy Contented Employees

"There is joy in work. There is no happiness except in the realization that we have accomplished something." Henry Ford

"It is all about quality of life and finding a happy balance between work and friends and family." Philip Green

"Happiness in the job puts excellence in the work." Aristotle

© Michael Bridgman

There is a serious shortage of qualified skilled workers in almost every industry and it is projected to get much worse since we as a country are not training enough people in skilled jobs.

Hopefully, with some of the ideas in this book, companies will find methods that can reduce turnover and make a better life for their workers. Companies that are providing a more attractive work environment also find it easier to attract new candidates.

In my opinion, difficulties between management and workers that make everyone unhappy are one of the leading causes for inferior performance and have cost companies wide-ranging losses. Unhappy employees at any level do not perform well. No one doubts that profits are lost when employees don't

© Michael Bridgman

perform at their peak and without sufficient profits companies can cease to exist. Companies tend to ignore employee problems if they are making profits. So, some companies never know their full profit potential when they do not fix problems. It is amazing to see how much hidden money is available when employee production is at its peak.

By using increased profits as the motive for management to act, I want to give companies the management tools to provide for an enjoyable and fulfilling work environment that will ultimately provide a better life for everyone throughout the company. When people work together toward a common goal more profits are the natural result. Am I reaching for the stars? Not really, I already proved many times that it can be done.

© Michael Bridgman

I have met managers, workers, and drivers from all over the USA and Canada who enjoy what they are doing but are unhappy over the treatment they get from their management. I have witnessed management that does not know how to manage employee activity appropriately is such a common problem that it seems to take place just about everywhere. The management style of "you have to do it because I say so" is often contrary to what loyal dedicated employees know from hands on experience. It can be very distressing to be told that something must be carried out a certain way simply because a manager said so, especially when there is obviously a more productive procedure that is available and ignored. Usually people at all levels want to be part of a solution and it is the people doing the

© Michael Bridgman

actual work that more often have the best solution.

According to the US Department of Labor, Bureau of Labor Statistics, the average adult during their working life spend more than a third of their life's time on the job. Life is short! So, living any part of this short life unhappy and unfulfilled is unnecessary and in some cases just plain torturous. It doesn't have to be that way. This book was written to show a way that could provide a better working life for everyone.

With Brio, I created a successful company with happy fulfilled employees doing everything the right way. So, what does it take? Obviously, there are several factors that go into running a successful business, but with all the things that must be done to succeed there is

© Michael Bridgman

one factor that is too often overlooked yet I feel is the one of the most important factors for a company's success. That factor is the mindset of the employees toward their company, coworkers, job performance and themselves. It seems to me that too many companies avoid dealing with the good or bad human reactions to the working conditions. It's not hard to provide a positive work environment that establishes happy employees which in turn can increase profits to the highest level possible for the company while providing for a more rewarding life for everyone.

There is a very large industry made up of consultants, motivators, seminars, and programs that offer ways to improve employee productivity. There are process applications and software that deal with how to cut costs,

© Michael Bridgman

improve efficiencies, lower turnover, increase productivity, hire better candidates, and a multitude of other employee and operational performance issues. But many of them fall short in providing the environment for a positive mindset. A positive mindset is a result of what I like to call "the human reaction factor" and without a positive human reaction to conditions these programs are generally unable to maximize their cost controlling value.

I have found that to be successful in improving work performance you will need to apply a process that is adaptable to circumstances within a company by industry segment, occupation, and work environment. You need to become familiar with the different beliefs and motivations of the individuals so

© Michael Bridgman

you can replace their individual thinking with a group centered sense of mission. Many people need something in common to connect with each other and a group goal is one of the common elements that brings everyone together. When you target personal performance toward a group goal you might avoid all the time and energy lost to programs and analysis that provide information but lack an actionable plan.

Some people say it is difficult to communicate that sense of mission especially with remote field workers that are outside of the day to day activities taking place in a central facility. I don't agree with that. For example, one of the companies where we put my methods in place, we were successful with remote field workers by using daily updates on

© Michael Bridgman

the company call-in line along with weekly fifteen to thirty-minute conference calls with the workers, managers, and team leaders from around the country all together on the same call. Everyone was in the loop and fully informed on what was going on companywide. If an employee was not available for the conference call, they could call in later and hear the recording. After listening to the recording, they could then leave comments in voice mail and those comments would then be discussed on the next conference call.

I have been observing all sorts of employee problems and management misunderstandings my whole working career. There are times when these situations have been truly heartbreaking. The workplace does not have to be a "house of torture." It should be a place

© Michael Bridgman

where people enjoy going and where they can fulfill their personal objectives of companionship, self-satisfaction, fun, and taking care of their family.

I created the processes by trying different ideas and evaluating what worked and what didn't work. I learned a lot from these early experiments and have learned a lot more during the past twenty-five years. Frankly, I was often surprised with the reactions from ideas that I thought would have a positive result and other ideas that I didn't think would work as well as they did. For example, I found out that service to others, pride in accomplishment, and being appreciated are much stronger performance motivators than money. In fact, money used as an incentive

© Michael Bridgman

can become an undesirable influence if not properly applied.

The techniques I present in this book are tried and true and have been proven to achieve results through actual experience. These processes are also quite simple and logical. As I developed different methods to deal with behavior, I found that basic human nature is inherently the same with all of us. What makes us different from each other is the way our childhood and adolescent experiences mold our individual way of thinking. Our way of thinking becomes our belief system. It's our unique belief systems developed from childhood that causes us to react to circumstances differently. Many times, our reactions are not in our own best interest from a societal point of view.

© Michael Bridgman

A process I developed that brings each of us back into harmony with each other and society is to provide a method for returning to our inborn natural childhood propensities of honesty, happiness, and sociable relationships. Did you ever notice how young children seem to find it easy to be happy, friendly, laugh, and have fun? All you need to do is watch preschool children at a daycare center interact with each other on a playground. You will see that happiness and having fun is a natural way to behave. Occasionally disputes arise, but if a daycare worker has the two kids express their differences with each other using the right technique they will often work out their own compromise.

As an employer, you can take advantage of this natural tendency to be happy, because no

© Michael Bridgman

matter how old we get we never lose that childhood desire to be happy. We are not born lazy, fearful, irresponsible, dishonest, hateful, and angry. These are unnatural self-destructive behaviors that we develop from our observations and experiences. In other words, we must be taught to behave badly. Kids don't have to learn how to be honest and happy because it's natural.

Do you remember Art Linkletter and his TV program "Kids say the darndest things"? The show was an excellent demonstration of the natural tendency to be honest. Go to YouTube and watch some of his shows. They are entertaining and proof of innocent honesty and happiness that comes naturally. Children must learn how to be dishonest, fearful and self-destructive. Since these behaviors are not

© Michael Bridgman

natural, it can be feasible to establish conditions in the work environment that can replace the noncompliant behaviors with responsible natural honesty and happiness.

Once you get rid of negative behavior, you can develop a group of happy, productive employees all working toward a common goal of accomplishment. I should caution that in some situations people refuse to adapt to the group behavior and must be removed from the group. If they are not removed their bad behavior will spread through the group and nullify your efforts.

These processes are built upon four fundamental realities of conduct.

1. Everything a person does always influences someone else.

114

© Michael Bridgman

2. We are socially interdependent with each other.

3. Attitude – A good attitude initiates good behavior providing good results. A bad attitude initiates bad behavior which will inherently provide adverse results.

4. Our personal world reflects our attitude towards it. What we give is what we get.

Excellence comes from people that enjoy their work. So, if you want to achieve excellence among your employees, you need to build conditions that prevent people from becoming unhappy. In other words, find out what conditions are causing the unhappiness and remove or change the unhappy causing conditions. Also in this process, you may need to counsel some unhappy individuals their way

© Michael Bridgman

back to their naturally happiness state of mind, or if that doesn't work show them out the door.

Happiness is an attitude and attitudes compel our actions. Attitudes are also infectious and can change the behavior of everyone in a group. The ancient Greek philosopher Aristotle once wrote *"the happy life is thought to be one of excellence; now an excellent life requires exertion and does not consist in amusement."* What I think he might be saying is that happiness does not come from jokes and laughter. Genuine happiness comes from achievement, and most importantly from our inner self. Vince Lombardi once said, *"the quality of a person's life is in direct proportion to their commitment to excellence, regardless of their chosen field of*

116

© Michael Bridgman

endeavor." Happiness and excellence go hand in hand.

I remember watching what appeared to be a three-year-old girl follow her mother into a store. The mother was excessively overweight and as a result rocked side to side when she walked. The little girl was not overweight but walked behind her mother, while using the same side to side motion. She was most likely too young to be mocking her mother. It was apparent to me it was just her mother unintentionally teaching her how to walk. With two children of my own and four grandchildren, I have continually noticed how children follow closely to the actions of adults as a way of learning how to behave. It looked to me like this little girl was walking exactly the

117

© Michael Bridgman

way her mother was inadvertently teaching her to walk.

The natural childhood tendency to learn by watching others stays with us throughout our life. In fact, we are constantly setting examples for each other by our behavior. What I found is that when a foreman exhibited professional behavior, and showed pride in his job and the company, the rest of the crew followed the example set by the foreman and became much more professional themselves. I have proved this time and again at my contracting company. The result was a sort of natural pride in self that translated into pride in the company and its mission.

As we grow into adulthood and reach the age of reason and accountability, we must

© Michael Bridgman

make choices for right and wrong. We often find we must overcome misguided childhood perceptions, which we learned from others. Then when we reach the "age of accountability" and become adults, we realize many of these youthful perceptions are disadvantageous to living a secure and satisfactory life. On the other hand, some of us lucky ones have good upbringing and are raised with all the characteristics we need to live a life of satisfaction and conformity. But no matter how we are raised, when we become adults we are in full control and make our own choices. As imperfect human beings, some of our choices are good and some are bad. What should steer us toward making good decisions is reconciling with the results of our bad decisions. However, sometimes it's difficult to acknowledge

© Michael Bridgman

responsibility for bad decisions. For some people, it is never their fault when something goes wrong. People that don't accept responsibility often don't improve and will continue to make bad decisions. Unfortunately, bad decisions don't just affect the person responsible, but they can also affect the people that have any connection with that failed person or the regrettable outcome of the decision.

Many have heard the story of the identical twin brothers that were raised by an irresponsible abusive alcoholic father that could never keep a job. One brother grew up to become just like his father and the other brother grew up to become a responsible and successful family man with a good job. When

© Michael Bridgman

the brother that turned out to be an irresponsible abusive alcoholic like his father, was asked why he did all the wrong things in life he said, *"what do you expect from someone who grew up with a father like I had."* When the other brother that turned out to be a responsible and successful family man was asked the secret to his success his response was, *"I simply learned what my father taught me about what <u>not</u> to do, and applied what he taught me to my life."* So, by changing your thoughts you change your behavior. Simply put, you can guide employee thoughts by controlling the work environment through the understanding of natural predispositions and ultimately affect employee performance.

© Michael Bridgman

As I said earlier, the market is full of employee productivity improvement type programs and processes. For many years, I have observed the effects of several of these programs and all the ones I have observed are management tools that by design avoid any direct decision making with the very employees that the program is intended to improve. For the most part, these programs involve employee work assessments from manager observations and performance statistics. I know of one company that covertly follows employees and video tapes them while they are performing their duties. Warehouse personnel are watched and taped inside the warehouse. Drivers are videotaped driving on the highway noting speed and lane changes etc. They are also videotaped while maneuvering the truck

© Michael Bridgman

into a loading dock to see if all the "Get Out And Look" (GOAL) procedures were followed. Unloading and handling of the freight and getting in and out of the truck are all videotaped. The videos are then used in evaluations. It's rare that the employee ever finds out that they were videotaped unless there is a flagrant violation.

Frequently these programs result in new rules, policies, and guidelines that the employees must agree to, and that are implemented without any direct employee participation. The reaction to the changes is often a negative one because of a natural tendency to resist change, or in some cases, the reaction is downright resentment. However, when the employees are involved and a

© Michael Bridgman

consensus is agreed to for the changes, the results are much more effective. Programs cannot fully succeed without the understanding and full acceptance of everyone from management to worker.

There are several methods I have tried that will put people on the right path for making decisions which are good for the company. I will be discussing these methods in the next chapter. But you must keep in mind that whatever changes you implement, they must be good for the company, good for the employees as a group, and ultimately good for the individuals. Processes will not work if they don't have a positive effect across the board. Keep in mind that human reaction to situations is fundamentally predictable.

© Michael Bridgman

As I've said, the interactions between management and workers establishes the circumstances for a positive or negative human response to everyone's job. Ultimately, it's all about the person's attitude or mindset toward their company, supervision, co-workers, and most importantly their individual self.

© Michael Bridgman

Chapter Five

Negative Enforcement Verses

Positive Influence.

"I think when I look out and I see there's so much negativity in the world and a lot of people are unhappy and a lot people are anxious, it just feels like that's one view of the world. But you don't have to always focus on that view of the world." Chris Hardwick

"The key to successful leadership today is influence, not authority." Ken Blanchard

"One of the best ways to influence people is to make them feel important." Roy T. Bennett

© Michael Bridgman

Let me start out by saying that most people want to have job security. They also understand that for the most part job security comes from doing a good job. Accordingly, employees understand that it is in their own best interest to be working for a successful employer. But when employees feel mistreated, their bad feelings become their focus and they lose interest in their employer's success. Bad management decisions cause conflict that effect everyone involved and in many cases the entire company.

My purpose in writing this book is to show the reader that there is a better way to do business. Results can be extraordinary when people work together for a greater good other than their selves and I've proved it many times.

© Michael Bridgman

Workers that are not happy with their managers tend to leave. Too often it is the best workers that can easily find another job that move on. Unnecessary high rates of turnover create substantial expense and are often not fully understood. There seems to be a universal concept that to get the best out of employees you must have power over their behavior. Companies use all sorts of control techniques from dismissal for rule violations to fancy computer software used to evaluate performance. These control techniques by their very nature provide limited success because they are based in negative enforcement. In other words, they punish poor or substandard behavior. The human reaction is to feel resentful when they are reprimanded and employee cooperation is lost. A more effective

© Michael Bridgman

process is to use an approach that promotes team work toward a common goal with rewards of accomplishment and recognition. People will discipline themselves and each other when properly motivated to achieve a greater goal beyond serving self. Standards of performance still must be set and adhered to, but when group goals are agreed upon and properly applied the enforcement of doing things right will come from the employees themselves.

Believe it or not, rewards of money by itself do not work. I know I've tried. What I have found that does work is satisfaction from achieving results, team level cooperation with co-workers, being valued, made to feel important, and satisfaction from helping others. These are much more effective motivators than money.

129

© Michael Bridgman

My employees at Brio for the most part wanted to do everything the right way simply because they believed that doing things the right way was better for the company, which in turn gave them more job security. I was always impressed at how conscientious and proud my employees were when they felt they were an important part of the company's success, and that their success came from the company being successful.

Many of my employees wore their company baseball cap when not working because of that pride. This would cause people to sometimes ask them about the company. They would proudly tell them all about what they did and the buildings they worked on. We were fortunate to work on a lot of prestigious

© Michael Bridgman

buildings such as Watergate Office Buildings 1 & 2 in Washington DC, Baltimore Hilton Towers, Bank of America Center in Norfolk, and many others. Knowing the status of our jobs some of the men collected the different customer's lapel pins and would pin them on their "dress hats" as they called them to display the significance of the buildings they worked on. When you have this much pride in your company and the work your company provides, the professionalism of the employee's shows throughout the company from the cleanliness of the trucks to the condition of the equipment, tools, and worksite. It also showed in the interaction with the building's tenants on the ground and when we rode the elevators to move the swing scaffold. I regularly received compliments from our customers because of

131

© Michael Bridgman

the praise our customers received from their tenants. The real bonus for everyone was that after the first three years in business, I never had to solicit new jobs. All my new work came to me from existing customers and referrals, so we consistently had a job waiting for a startup when a current job was completed. Companies need to maximize profits to stay competitive. As I have said throughout this book, the best way to maximize profits is to create a happy fun work environment. Maximum profits are obtained when you have employees that are having fun doing their job.

A prevalent damaging condition, which I have seen many times over, is poor communication. When the manager attempts to communicate to the worker what needs to

© Michael Bridgman

be done, the manager is often not specific as to what is expected. Frequently a manager expects a worker to do their tasks a certain way but hasn't communicated their expectations properly to the worker. Then since the worker did not have specific instructions, they must go about completing the task by making their own decisions on what should be done. Then the manager sees the worker making their own decisions without management approval. Too often the result is the worker being criticized by the manager because the manager felt a loss of control and not necessarily because the work wasn't getting done properly and on schedule. I have seen good workers resign due to poor communication and unfounded criticism.

© Michael Bridgman

The other problem that contributes to poor communication is due to hiring managers fresh out of college without experience and suddenly these managers are managing a group of workers, without any idea of what is involved in doing the work. The worker's behavior tanks when receiving unwise or deficient instructions from an ignorant manager.

In my opinion, the two worst attributes a manager can have, are ignorance with arrogance and unfortunately many of today's college kids fall squarely into those two modes of behavior. Communication must be complete, concise, and fully understood by politely asking for something to be done. I never told my employees to do anything. I always asked

© Michael Bridgman

my employees. I never used words like "I need you to" or "you have to" or "I expect you to." Instead, I always asked "do you mind" or "would you" or "can you" or "could you help", which are much more effective than a demand.

When people feel they are being treated unfairly, they may tend to behave with a mind set to "balance the scales" as one worker put it to me. This "I'll get even attitude" can mean many things. Some of the common consequences are:

1. Filthy work areas.

2. Needed equipment repairs not being turned in to get fixed.

3. Tardiness and unexcused absences.

4. Care-less job performance (very costly for some companies especially with safety).

5. Pilfering of company property.

135

© Michael Bridgman

6. Deception, (inflated time cards and overstated expenses, revealing trade secrets, and falsified worker's compensation claims).

7. Poor customer relations and service failures (companies have gone out of business with this problem alone).

The behaviors listed above are not exclusive of each other. For example; when you discover a problem with overstated expenses you will probably find that there are varying degrees of the other problem behaviors taking place as well. However, when you have employees that trust each other and their management, feel appreciated, and have pride in their employer, then the "get even attitude" disappears. Workers will watch over each other and

© Michael Bridgman

managers will watch over other managers all in support of the company.

As an example, while at a customer's location with my contracting company, I was observing from a distance a job site cleanup at the end of the day when a new hire simply threw the cables and tools in the back of the truck. The truck had been set up so that there was a designated place to store everything. When the supervisor saw what the new hire was doing, the supervisor asked the new hire to put everything in its place and not leave it in a heap in the back of the truck. The new hire said *"what's the difference? We just have to get everything out tomorrow any way."* The supervisor said, "that's not the way we do it here" and started putting everything in its place himself. Putting the equipment in their

137

© Michael Bridgman

proper storage place was a small effort and took about three minutes. After everything was put away it was discovered that an $450 electric hand held concrete chisel was missing. The new hire went back to the work area found the tool and put it in the truck. The supervisor said, "that's why we have a place for everything so we know for sure that we haven't missed something." The new hire never had a problem putting things away properly after that. Honest and purposeful, non-scolding communication, between the worker and the supervisor combined with the learning experience of the missing tool, reinforced why things needed to be done a certain way. When everyone understands each other's responsibilities, you create a condition of cooperation and team effort. When everyone is

© Michael Bridgman

working toward a common goal you can produce the extraordinary results that add directly to bottom line profits.

It goes without question that the best ideas for improving an organization's operating procedures often come from front-line workers who possess firsthand knowledge of the problems and how they can be resolved. But they often fail to speak up because they are not convinced of the value of doing so, and they fear personal risk of potential repercussions. What if the improvements could make a senior manager look bad by making the senior manager appear incompetent? Even without such fears, employees may not feel motivated to speak up particularly if they do not believe that anyone will care or respond to their concerns.

© Michael Bridgman

A team or group of people working together with a respected team leader can provide the support for speaking up and offering solutions to the problems since the team atmosphere will provide protection and corroboration, while at the same time give credit to the individual. Allowing employees to demonstrate their proposed solutions can also be particularly gratifying and rewarding for both management and workers. Employees appreciate and respond favorably to a management that values employee participation in solving problems and improving operational performance. In addition, employee involvement in offering solutions increases the potential to improve operational performance. Their firsthand knowledge enables them to understand the root causes of problems and

© Michael Bridgman

offer well-informed ideas on how to solve them. It's all about communication, expectation, work environment, and mission.

I remember one time we were installing a full tear off replacement roof on a fifteen story Holiday Inn. It was a very hot summer day on the way to over 100°. The hotel management did not want the noise and work activity to disturb the guests while they were in their rooms, so we were limited to working from 8:30am to 4:30pm. A hot 100°+ day meant that it was unsafe to work past 1:00 pm. Yet, we still had a deadline for completion. When temperatures are high with the bright sun's heat bearing down on the roof of a fifteen-story building, work conditions become unbearable past noon. We always had cold soda and water in an ice chest so anyone could stop and get a

141

© Michael Bridgman

drink anytime. But with weather as hot as it was, heat stroke was still a possibility. When you combine a deadline for completion, limited work time available, and work that was very physical and dirty, you could expect people to be very unhappy and want to quit. On this day, I arrived on the job around 12:30 and told all the workers to knock off for the day due to the heat. Believe it or not, to my surprise they wanted to keep working. My foreman came to me and said he enjoyed working for me more than going home and would be glad to stay on the job despite the heat. But, I insisted that I didn't want anyone getting sick and told all of them to quit for the day. Guess what! Because of the positive behaviors of the employees, we were still able to stay on schedule and complete the work on time and under the labor

© Michael Bridgman

budget even with two lost half work days. The reason we could stay on schedule was because my crews were happy to work on a Saturday to make up for the half days we lost to heat.

There was a time when we had a big ten month long job in Norfolk, VA. When we were half way toward the job completion, everything was progressing right on schedule and the quality of the work was extraordinary. So, I decided to take everyone out to dinner as a sort of celebration for their outstanding performance. As always, since pizza and beer were their two favorite foods, everyone wanted to go to an Italian style pizza restaurant with its friendly neighborly atmosphere. We would have tables put together so we could all sit across from each other and have the food served family style. I happen to like anchovies

143

© Michael Bridgman

on my pizza. But no one else liked them, so typically I would order one large pizza with anchovies on it. The problem was that if I could not eat it all, the leftover would go uneaten. (Between you and I, my employees didn't always know that I would usually take the left-over pizza with me to eat later, so I could enjoy the cold pizza and the anchovies.) On this occasion before the restaurant took our orders, I was presented a large can of anchovies to put on any pizza I wanted. They told me that they wanted to avoid the expense of buying a whole pizza with anchovies on it that only I would eat. I thanked them, and really enjoyed the anchovies even though I missed the option of the cold pizza later. After thinking about the incident with the anchovies it came to my mind that they really did feel a

© Michael Bridgman

sense of ownership in the company and didn't want to see any money squandered.

There are a limited number of high rise buildings in any one area so we traveled away from home regularly. Since we usually had at least one local job around the Baltimore and Washington, DC area in progress, I could rotate the crews on less technical jobs so they would be local for two weeks and out of town for two weeks. This reduced the family hardship of being away from home. When we had long term out of town jobs lasting six months or more, I would rent a house and pay a meal per-diem. On shorter term jobs, I would get a good rate for upscale hotel rooms for a few weeks, which I would negotiate a cost just slightly more than a cheap motel. Rooms in the upscale hotels were highly appreciated by the

© Michael Bridgman

workers. When we stayed in hotels I paid for actual meals and expenses within the IRS limits. I must say that my generosity was never abused even though I did not control where or what they could eat. I feel the reason there was no abuse was because my employees were looking at the big picture of what was good for the company was good for them.

Employees want to give back to their company when they are appreciated and feel that their contribution to the company is their personal part of the big picture. They get more work done, come up with more new ideas, and create more value. When the feelings of ownership are instilled into the mindset the results are truly extraordinary.

© Michael Bridgman

Some additional benefits are listed as follows:

1. Employees become more accountable and accept more responsibility.

2. Employees will reduce or eliminate unacceptable behavior of others through self-enforcement.

3. A mutually supportive company culture reduces turnover and provides an environment that attracts more talented higher performing employees. I always had a waiting list of people wanting to work for us largely because of referrals.

4. A shared mission partnership between employees and management is easily instilled.

© Michael Bridgman

5. Teamwork comes about from goals and objectives that are shared. A shared cause and a shared goal establish the conditions success.

6. Happy employees are healthier and more motivated giving us a competitive advantage by being more productive.

Simply put, you should have a good reaction from being good to the employees and you may get a bad reaction from being bad or indifferent to the employees. It always boils down to the "human reaction factor."

© Michael Bridgman

Chapter Six

The Discovery Procedure

"You never discover the unexpected if you always stick with the familiar."
Jeff Dixon

"We don't receive wisdom we must discover it for ourselves."
Marcel Proust

"What is wanted is not the will to believe, but the will to find out, which is the exact opposite."
Bertrand Russell

© Michael Bridgman

The process to establish openness for group involvement starts with the natural human response of adaptation to the environment. So, first you should identify both the negative and positive conditions. In other words, you want to know what to fix. Positive conditions are usually obvious and readily identified. On the other hand, negative conditions are often hard to uncover and range from the mundane of a work space being too hot or cold to a serious problem with a demanding manager that everyone dreads. A good way to find out what is initiating their behaviors is to use a process of observation and employee interviews. Each company has different issues, so you may want find out what is specifically needed to improve productivity. You may also want to know how different personalities work together.

© Michael Bridgman

Confidential interviews conducted by an impartial third party without any connections to employees or management are the most effective way I know of to obtain the information that will allow you to discover the specific changes needed for making improvements. When data collected from these interviews is categorized and prioritized you can build a clear pattern that will help in implementing change and ultimately forming policy.

Before I go into more on the discovery process of finding deficiencies, I need to interject that this is the one course of action that is in the most danger of being shut down before it even begins. It is not uncommon for senior managers in larger companies to create an independent vertical self-contained

151

© Michael Bridgman

management organization within their group which is commonly referred to as a silo. Silos are created primarily for job protection where information about problems and mismanagement are kept away from the rest of the company. In other words, you watch my back and I will watch yours. People are expected to have as little contact as possible with people outside of their silo by working and communicating only with the people inside their silo. The effect of silos is that innovation and improvement is hindered because the silo chain of command doesn't want anyone finding out what may be going on. Additionally, minor silos are often created within silos and these stymie potential improvements even further. A longtime manager once said to me that the only way he has survived in the company was

© Michael Bridgman

by keeping his head down and out of notice. A vice president in a company I was working with described these senior management silos as kingdoms and the minor silos as princedoms.

So, it is important to know that trying to initiate a program of any sort can intimidate the managers that created or inherited the silos. These managers will make every effort to prevent implementation of the improvements or will at least try to minimize and discredit any information derived from the interviews if in any way the managers are shown in a bad light. This means that the order to begin must come from the very top of the organization with a definitive plan for follow up, enforcement, and control of the process.

© Michael Bridgman

During this discovery phase with the employees, it is also good to talk with customers to find out what the weaknesses and strengths are from the customer perspective. It is not uncommon for long time customers to know more about the inner workings of a company than the company management. I have also found that when conducting the interviews with the employees the employees often feel better about the company when they sense that somebody cares about their concerns. Customers also feel better about the company when they know that their concerns are being addressed as well.

Once identified, you develop and install a course of action that replaces the negative conditions with positive conditions. I call this

© Michael Bridgman

the application of the "human reaction factor." Simply put, when negative conditions are identified and replaced with positive conditions, the employees will respond appropriately and the company can then reap the benefits of confident, upbeat, and better performing employees.

Another effective method I have used to find out where changes need to be made is the resolution manager method. This is a very effective technique for discovery and it is also effective for giving employees confidence that the company really wants to improve things for everyone. This method is simply a hotline that employees at all levels can use confidentially to call in about concerns. If employees don't trust that their reports will remain confidential, you can establish the hotline by using an

© Michael Bridgman

independent third party offsite so that confidentiality can be assured with confidence.

As an offsite process, this can be the most effective procedure to use when managers have created walls of protection or silos within their area of responsibility. As I mentioned earlier, silos are created to exert absolute authority without interference. They are also created to protect the managers within the silo from revelations of mishandled management. The problem is silos provide a way for managers to corrupt their power and in my experience these managers will do almost anything to protect that power. So, you may not get an honest assessment of the problems without an absolute guarantee of confidentiality when conducting the call-in interviews.

© Michael Bridgman

Four components will increase the chances for success using this method of discovery.

1. A call-in number or email with guaranteed confidentiality so that anyone calling in will be able to speak freely without fear of retribution. People can be encouraged to use off site pay phones with a free 800 number to improve confidence that their call is truly confidential. It is also important that no one is to know anything about the information derived from these calls until after they are reviewed with the top executives.

2. All information from these calls needs to be categorized by group type and frequency which is useful in establishing a pattern of problems.

© Michael Bridgman

3. All decisions on changes that are made because of the calls must be decided at the very top of the executive level which means the CEO or an executive committee headed by the CEO.

4. As a follow-up to monitoring the changes, it is prudent to install a Workers Advisory Council made up of workers, line supervisors and carefully selected managers to advise executive management. To be effective it's necessary to provide for all levels of worker and management involvement in decisions and fine-tuning of the policy changes. Policy changes that result from the information obtained should remain ongoing. These ongoing policy changes will discourage the potential to return to

© Michael Bridgman

the old ways and lose the advantages gained by making the changes.

© Michael Bridgman

Chapter Seven

The Corporate Culture

"A company is stronger if it is bound by love rather than by fear." Herb Kelleher

"The greatest force of nature is people standing shoulder to shoulder walking in the same direction." Lynn Tilton

"It is literally true that you can succeed best and quickest by helping others succeed."

Napoleon Hill

The management philosophy is what creates the culture for a company's greatness.

© Michael Bridgman

Southwest Airlines continually proves how the effectiveness of establishing a fun, supporting environment that translates into happy employees. Happy employees initiate happy loyal customers which maximize profits and company success. There are many very successful companies that continually out perform their peers because of a corporate culture that provides for happy employees doing exceptional jobs.

As I said earlier, Brio Industries was a specialty contractor performing high rise sidewall remedial waterproofing. This meant that I had to hire people that were not afraid of working on a building 300 feet high, while standing on a swing scaffold hanging outside on the side the building. I quickly found out that most construction workers were not

© Michael Bridgman

suited for this type of work. I also found that the person that could handle the heights was often a very independent personality type and not easily managed. They also had a little bit of daredevil in them and were sometimes not interested in following all the required safety rules. Basically, I found myself hiring a bunch of rebels.

Since safety, work ethic, and responsibility all come from behavior, I integrated behavior accountability and attitude into the process of building my dream team. Listed below are some of the principals I used to instill these qualities by using the human reaction factor techniques.

The six qualities listed on the next page became the foundation for establishing our company culture.

162

© Michael Bridgman

1. Right is right, and wrong is wrong. You do the right thing and you get the right result and when you do the wrong thing you get the wrong result. Simple, isn't it!

2. Working safe is not an option. Your safety is important not only to yourself, "injuries hurt and pain is not fun", but safety is also important to your family, co-workers, and the viability of the company that employs you.

3. People like doing business with happy, considerate people. Pleasantly greet all people you encounter. Do not make anyone uncomfortable. When your clients are happy with you, they tend to want to stay happy and will continue to do business with you. Happy, satisfied clients are what keep you employed.

© Michael Bridgman

4. We are individuals that together are one company. People don't see Drew, Brian, or Don when they see you on the job, they see Brio Industries, which means any bad behavior by one can cost everyone, not just the person behaving badly.

5. Everyone has an important role in getting the job done right and on schedule. We all need each other, so I always encouraged openness for suggestions. Any concerns were addressed immediately by the supervisors and by me when necessary.

6. The team atmosphere of working together with openness eliminated complaints and bad behaviors, simply because all concerns were addressed.

164

© Michael Bridgman

As I previously mentioned in chapter three, I was selected as one of twelve truck drivers to represent the trucking industry to the public by being appointed as a Captain with the 2001-2003 America's Road Team. One of the events I participated in was a student hiring fair for high school and college students. I represented the trucking industry as a career choice, along with about fifty other participating companies from various industries. Directly next to my table was the table for Southwest Airlines. I must tell you, that I have more respect for the Southwest Airlines business philosophy than I do for any other company. I was flying on Southwest by choice early on before they had any flights east of the Mississippi River.

© Michael Bridgman

During the time of this student hiring fair, I was flying several times per month and I truthfully told the Southwest Recruiter that I always go out of my way to fly with Southwest. The reason I like to fly with Southwest is because I always have a good experience. So, I asked the recruiter what was the Southwest secret to hiring efficient, good-natured people. His reply was that there is one critical quality that Southwest requires a person to have before an interview is granted. Without this quality, there is absolutely no chance that person will be hired. What do you think this quality is? The answer is "A SMILE"! According to this recruiter, an applicant without a genuine friendly smile when being greeted is simply not considered regardless of the position or that person's background. Simply

© Michael Bridgman

put Southwest hires only people that possess a naturally happy disposition. This happiness requirement is the basis for their "customer first" or making the customer happy culture. The other secret is the positive support from management that keeps Southwest employees in high spirits really enjoying their jobs and showing their joy in the way they perform. Employees have fun working at Southwest and that translates into customers having fun along with the employees.

Business travelers know that Southwest continues to make substantial profits while many of the other airlines are struggling to survive. They also are rated by the travel industry as having the most on time flights and the highest rated customer service. In my opinion, Southwest achieves their superior

© Michael Bridgman

performance because of a "happy employee/customer first" culture. Southwest's corporate culture demonstrates that a company's performance is a result of the employee's performance. Southwest thrives because people like to be happy and this happy experience is a direct result of Southwest's employees happily performing their jobs.

There is a Southwest Airlines news release on the internet that reviews the history of Herb Kelleher and how Southwest Airlines has grown since it started. The following excerpt from that release says it all concerning how effective the Southwest happiness culture has been and continues to be.

© Michael Bridgman

Southwest commenced service with three airplanes in 1971 and in May of 2008, when Kelleher stepped down as Executive Chairman, Southwest operated a fleet of more than 527 airplanes and performed more than 3,400 flights per day. Kelleher's Company has been profitable for 38 consecutive years; has never furloughed an Employee; and today carries the most originating domestic passengers of any U.S. airline. The Fall 2002 edition of Money *magazine revealed that, during the 30-year period 1972-2002, Southwest produced the highest return to shareholders of any company included in the S&P 500 during that 30-year period: $10,000 invested in Southwest in 1972 was worth $10,200,000 in 2002 (an average increase of 25.99% per year).*

169

The Transport Workers Union National President Jim Little announced on behalf of local TWU 550, 555, and 556 that, in an unprecedented action, "Herb Kelleher was now an honorary lifetime member of the TWU in grateful appreciation for [his] unparalleled Leadership in creating a magnificent airline and a generation of Employees who love coming to work." (December 2008)

No doubt most of us are aware of companies that were driven out of business because of deficient employee performance while at the same time their competition thrived. Let's expand on the Southwest experience. I have flown often observing firsthand the different levels of service I receive from the various airlines. As I said earlier, I can honestly say that every time I have flown

170

© Michael Bridgman

with Southwest I get off the flight feeling good. The other airlines don't always give me that good feeling. In fact, there have been times that I couldn't wait to get off the plane. I like feeling good better than feeling bad and that's why I do everything in my power to fly with Southwest. I have met many other Southwest customers that feel like I do. Southwest's success is in part, a result of happy employees serving happy customers. I am persistently dumbfounded why other struggling airlines don't apply Southwest's happiness culture to their own operations.

I'll never forget a time when I flew in to Baltimore from Chicago on a flight where I had been given a complimentary upgrade to first class. The upgrade was nice but I still didn't get the smiles and good feelings I get on

© Michael Bridgman

Southwest. I insisted that our travel department put me on Southwest going back. So, two days later I had the flight I wanted on Southwest going back to Chicago. When I walked on the Southwest plane I asked the attendant if they had a first-class section since I had a first-class seat on the flight coming in. (Just so you know I was aware that Southwest seats were all the same class and they did not have a first-class section on any of their planes). Her reply was *"yes sir! we certainly do have a first-class section.* Surprised! I said, *"you do! Where?"* Her reply was a classic. She said, *"the whole plane is first class sir."* I agreed with her, not because of the seats but because of the service.

I was fortunate to have been able to develop a friendship with a customer in Norfolk, VA

© Michael Bridgman

that was worth over a million dollars in business. We cooperated with each other to an extraordinary degree. I invited him to lunch on several occasions to strengthen the friendship and show him how grateful I was to have him as a customer. On one occasion, I took him to an upscale seafood restaurant with a waterside outdoor patio. The food here was as fresh as it gets and expertly prepared. This restaurant was extremely popular so you could not get a table without a reservation. My customer was very happy about my choice of this restaurant when I extended the invitation. While enjoying our fantastic lunch, I told him I picked this restaurant because I wanted to thank him in a special way for our friendship and all the business he gave me and my employees. He responded by saying, "that he should be

© Michael Bridgman

thanking me," because to have a contractor that always did great work at a good price and never that caused him any problems was a rare find for him. He went on to say that I made him look good to his superiors and he appreciated that more than I know. Then when the check came he insisted on paying for it. When I insisted that I wanted to pay for it, he told me I could cover the tip which I did.

I had never realized how important our work ethic and high standards were to him and how we made his job easier and made him look good to his superiors. It always comes back to everyone feeling good. I and my employees made him feel good and, in doing so, we had a customer for life if we continued to perform. When I told my employees about the lunch experience with the customer, they

174

© Michael Bridgman

really showed their pride and wanted to make sure they were doing their very best for our customer.

There is a lady by the name of Lynn Tilton who has become famous by buying distressed companies and returning them to viability. As a result, she has become a very successful billionaire. She asserts on her website that she has turned around companies that were on the brink of bankruptcy and in some cases about to go out of business. In turning around these companies, she has saved thousands of jobs. Her portfolio consists of more than 75 companies.

How is she able to turn around companies that in many cases were just about to go under? Obviously, there are numerous

© Michael Bridgman

factors that go into saving a company, such as financial and management restructuring. It is my opinion that she seems to also recognize the need to create a corporate environment that invigorates the employees. Apparently, she understands one of the important ingredients that go into providing for company's success is having innovative employees focused on doing what needs to be done to make the company prosperous. From all appearances, she knows how to produce a corporate culture within these companies that provides for happy employees striving toward excellence.

Another good example of phenomenal success is Google. Google's success is well known and truly extraordinary. Google goes to great lengths to provide an enjoyable experience for everyone involved in the

© Michael Bridgman

company. Google shows they care in many ways. Their perks include a free gourmet cafeteria, employee lounges, massage services, free laundry and dry cleaning, oil change service, personal concierge to place dinner reservations, weekly TGIF parties, and top-quality speakers visiting on a regular basis. Google's list goes on further.

Personally, I think these are great perks but they are much more than I feel is necessary. You don't have to have an abundance of perks to have hard working dedicated employees. As a point to back up the position of not needing an abundance of perks, my employees at Brio said to me that the people they work with and the work that they accomplish are the two best elements of the job. At Brio, we had instilled a culture of

177

© Michael Bridgman

friends working together in support of each other while having a good time. However, I learned that people do not develop respect for each other on their own. The respect for each other had to be established using a group centered mission and pride in accomplishment.

Friendship and company pride are very strong motivators. People who make friends with co-workers work harder and accomplish more because they are having fun spending time together and encouraging each other. I have often observed that a common influence for employee accomplishment often comes from the interaction between the individuals within the company. Everyone influences each other and that influence is good for the company or not good for the company.

© Michael Bridgman

So, if it is known that one aspect of a company's success is often a result of happy employee's, then why don't more companies have a company culture that promotes a happy productive workforce?

On occasion, I mistakenly hired an egotistical self-serving type of person that did not want to be part of the group. These self-serving employees were generally trouble makers that tried to make themselves look good at the expense of the others. However, when the friendship environment is properly established and supported with effective leadership everyone becomes focused on the group's goals. The self-serving employees find themselves awkwardly out of place and in most cases either get on board with the program or end up leaving on their own to go to other jobs.

179

© Michael Bridgman

People who are not happy unless they are the center of attention simply do not fit in. At Brio, no one was the center of attention including me. We were all about what was best for everyone else. It was never about what was best for any one person. But, you know what was best for everyone was in fact also best for each individual. Selfish divisiveness simply had no place to exist.

As I said earlier, about 65% of my contracts with Brio were out of town. When my workers were out of town they tended to bond by spending their off time with each other. This created lasting friendships that translated into more cooperation between each other on the job. It is important to note that most of the time when the work environment does not encourage camaraderie on the job, the off-duty

© Michael Bridgman

behavior tends to be more self-centered. Each person tends to do their own thing and all behavior on or off the job becomes less controllable when individuals do not share responsibility to each other. This is where my attitude guidance on responsible behavior played an important role. Most of the time they spent their off-duty time together and their behavior was controlled by peer pressure. Occasionally some of them would go off on their own but they still behaved themselves because of lingering peer pressure and they did not want to disappoint their friends or me.

© Michael Bridgman

Chapter Eight

The Importance of Group Meetings.

My experience from working with people is that you can have a conversation with someone or have a meeting with a group of people, and from that meeting will derive an answer to a question that no individual could have ever thought of by him or herself. John C. Mather

When you focus on problems you will have more problems. When you focus on possibilities you'll have more opportunities. Kushandwizdom

It has been my experience that people are inherently resistant to

© Michael Bridgman

change. For changes to be effective, everyone should be agreeable to the changes. Group meetings are a technique to come together and achieve consensus to the changes. These meetings are also an effective way to establish a group centered mindset that can make the difference between a moderately successful transition and a transition that is outstandingly successful. Group meetings and seminars can become the glue that keeps all the changes for improvement in place and functioning.

Group meetings are not necessary in all situations. There are circumstances where it is next to impossible to have all the employees

© Michael Bridgman

attend. I mentioned in chapter four that conference calls with open discussion are effective especially when an employee is not available for the conference call they can call in later, hear the recording and leave voice mail comments to be included with the next conference call. Another method could be an internal blog site. No matter what you do, open and complete information covering all the changes is helpful for getting everyone in agreement. As I have stated several times, making sure that everyone in an organization is agreeable to the changes is important for the success of the changes.

Face to face group get-togethers with open discussion and exchange of

© Michael Bridgman

ideas will keep everyone's attention and most importantly establish the conditions for everyone to become agreeable participants with the changes. They are also an opportunity to provide training on various topics of job performance. I have been successful in using the seminar approach with open discussion to combine training and the announcement of the changes into one session.

The first meeting to take place should be with the executive level to decide and agree on what changes are needed as a result of the discovery process. Once the executive group decides on what changes need to be put in effect, you can establish the agenda

© Michael Bridgman

for the series of meetings informing all the employees down the chain of command what the changes are and why they are being implemented. The importance of including everyone in these meetings cannot be over emphasized.

I have learned that the consecutive group meetings work best when they are conducted as an informational training seminar with open discussion. Since the changes are based on the discovery process where everyone submitted their opinions and you are addressing everyone's concerns, it should be easy to find agreement for the changes. The meeting agenda also can include input on how to adapt to the changes.

© Michael Bridgman

Persuading the employee to change from a "me" mindset to a "we" mindset is a real challenge. Since mindset is an attitude and attitudes drive behavior y0u may want to explain to the employees that the changes may bring about a need to transform their behavior and routines. During these meetings, the meeting facilitator should impress the importance of understanding and appreciating the significance of each individual contribution to the success of the changes.

Establishing clearly defined goals that everyone can focus on is an effective component to establishing the group centered mindset. Without the group centered mindset, there is a greater

© Michael Bridgman

danger of individuals doing their own thing and causing disarray. This may sound trite, but when employees feel the love from their employer the cooperation expands to the maximum. As Herb Kelleher, the cofounder of Southwest Airlines, has said *"A company is stronger if it is bound by love rather than by fear."* When employees feel loved and appreciated they develop pride in their company, pride in their job, and ultimately pride in themselves. Pride goes a long way in creating the happy work environment. So, when it is all said and done, group meetings or seminar presentations can be the best way to establish group harmony although not the only way.

© Michael Bridgman

Chapter Nine

Now Is the Time for Action

"Vision without action is merely a dream. Action without vision just passes the time. Vision with action can change the world." Joel A. Barker

"There are risks and costs to action. But they are far less than the long-range risks of comfortable inaction." John F. Kennedy

"Take time to deliberate; but when the time for action arrives, stop thinking and go in."

189

© Michael Bridgman

Andrew Jackson

Always keep in mind that when you start putting changes in place you are almost certain to have to deal with diehards that will not go along with the changes. Especially where middle and upper level managers have always been able to do things their way and now they feel a loss of power and control.

I have found that the way to overcome resistance is to hold conferences starting at the executive level. You need to explain what was revealed during the discovery process and what was suggested from the participants to fix the discrepancies. Power point and graphs are useful to illustrate the information and provide more impact. Discussion can then ensue with

© Michael Bridgman

this information so goals and objectives can be agreed upon. After the executive group reaches consensus on the goals and objectives you need to hold conferences and discussions to reach agreement with the other levels of management and employees all the way down to the workers. Chapter eight goes into more detail on the best way to conduct the conferences. It is very important that everyone be on board and agreeable to the changes. The employee attitude should improve to a surprising level when they see action being taken. Holdouts against the improvements and employee empowerment will be out voted and will go along with the changes. However, you can expect that not everyone will be agreeable. So, to avoid the possibility of sabotage you

© Michael Bridgman

need to be careful and weed out anyone that is resisting.

I remember one case where a vice president and three others that worked under him resigned because they didn't like the empowerment given to subordinates. Their resignation was a gift for the company since they were major contributors to the discord that existed. As you move down through the layers of management with your conferences the number of resisters may increase. So be watchful of covert resistance. When everyone in an organization is onboard and allowed input into decisions the feeling of having suggestions recognized will bring about a renewed pride in the company and how they do their job. Once you firmly establish policy to support the improvements and the anxiety of

© Michael Bridgman

previous bad management is removed, worker engagement should improve.

I have learned that the most effective process for change is one that is adaptable to the specific conditions that are different with each company and each individual. Believe me when I say that a pure text book approach without adaptability will always have limited results. This may sound complicated, but it's not. The complication comes from those resisting the changes. When you eliminate the resistance, everything is simplified. The success comes from the employee involvement because it's the employees within their various departments that know where to improve conditions better that any outsider.

© Michael Bridgman

This book is a summary of my actual experience and not a scholarly work of theory and conjecture. I have lived through everything written in this book. Fortunately, my life has been remarkably varied and I have had the opportunity to prove to myself and to others that the advice I present in this book has worked for me on several occasions. In fact, the effectiveness of the changes often exceeded everyone's expectations.

If you really want to be working with a company that promotes employee happiness and your company was left at the starting gate, then this book can offer substantial advice for you. My view is that life is too short to live it in a state of anguish and suffering just because you need a job. To have an employee come to me say that they enjoy being on the job more

194

© Michael Bridgman

than going home is a great feeling for me and says a lot about the company culture.

My personal mission is to use my knowledge to contribute to a better workplace making companies and their employees more successful. I am always available if you the reader have any questions or want any help.

I have found that some people have trouble grasping the concepts and executing the processes. The procedures are not complicated for me and with my experience I have learned how to avoid the pitfalls and how to recognize and apply the actions that have the best chances for success.

Thank you for reading my book. My hope is that what you have read here will give you the

© Michael Bridgman

tools to create a superb workplace making a better life for everyone in your company.

Please don't hesitate to contact me at:

bridgman302@gmail.com

You have my blessings and best wishes.

Thank you.

© Michael Bridgman

Realities of Behavior

Five essentials to have happy employees

1. A sense of accomplishment.

2. Fellowship that results from shared goals.

3. Teamwork where people interact in support of each other.

4. Being respected.

5. Pride in the company and the company's mission.

Superior productivity and exceptional customer service are the natural results of happy employees. What more could a company ask for.

© Michael Bridgman

Four effects of conduct

1. Everything a person does always influences someone else.

2. We are socially interdependent with each other.

3. Attitude – A good attitude initiates good behavior providing good results. A bad attitude initiates bad behavior which will inherently provide adverse results.

4. Our personal world reflects our attitude towards it. What we give is what we get.

Excellence comes from happy people that enjoy their work. So, if you want to achieve excellence among your employees you should create conditions that prevent people from becoming unhappy.

© Michael Bridgman

Benefits of being appreciated

1. Employees become more accountable and accept more responsibility.

2. Employees will reduce or eliminate unacceptable behavior of others through self-enforcement.

3. A mutually supportive company culture reduces turnover and provides an environment that attracts more talented higher performing employees. I always had a waiting list of people wanting to work for us largely because of referrals.

4. A shared mission partnership between employees and management is easily instilled.

5. Teamwork comes about from goals and objectives that are shared. A shared cause and a shared goal establish the conditions for success.

© Michael Bridgman

6. Happy employees are healthier and more motivated giving us a competitive advantage by being more productive.

Simply put you will have a good reaction from being good to the employees and you get a bad reaction from being bad or indifferent to the employees. It always boils down to the "human reaction factor." Employees want to give back to their employer when they are appreciated.

© Michael Bridgman

INDEX

© Michael Bridgman

© Michael Bridgman

© Michael Bridgman

© Michael Bridgman

© Michael Bridgman

© Michael Bridgman

© Michael Bridgman

© Michael Bridgman

© Michael Bridgman

© Michael Bridgman

© Michael Bridgman

Roy T. Bennett, Page 131

© Michael Bridgman

© Michael Bridgman

© Michael Bridgman

www.ingramcontent.com/pod-product-compliance
Lightning Source LLC
Chambersburg PA
CBHW071422180526
45170CB00001B/181